KINGDOM

Photographs by:
Colin Jeal

Front cover painting by:
Julie Stooks

**To Geoff Izzard and
Joan Pearce, founders of the
modern Rat Fancy**

*The author and publishers would like to thank
the following:*

The National Fancy Rat Society
for permission to quote from the Standards

Hanards Pet Centre, Romsey

and Mavis Webb

Your First

FANCY RAT

CONTENTS

Introduction 4

Selection 6

Housing 11

General Care 14

Showing 18

Varieties 20

Breeding............24

Health 28

Bibliography......33

©1996
by Kingdom
Books
PO7 6AR
ENGLAND

your first fancy rat

Kingdom Books is an imprint of T.F.H. Publications   Printed in England.

INTRODUCTION

Rats belong to the scientific order **Rodentia**, the rodents, which evolved some 70 million years ago. Rodents are characterised by chisel-like teeth which they use very effectively for gnawing. Indeed, the name 'rodent' is derived from the Latin verb *rodere*, meaning 'to gnaw'. The two most common species of rat originated in Asia and belong to the genus *Rattus*. They are omnivorous scavengers, eating corn, wheat, insects, carrion, birds' eggs, human refuse - in short, just about anything.

Rattus rattus, the Black (or Ship) Rat, is usually black or dark brown. It is slender, with a pointed muzzle, large hairless ears and a long whiplash tail. It measures 35-40cm including the tail, and weighs 200-225 grams. The Black Rat became well established in Europe as far back as the first century AD. It is most (in)famous as the carrier of bubonic plague (the Black Death) which devastated the population of Europe during the Middle Ages.

Rattus norvegicus, the Brown (or Norway) Rat, has a blunter muzzle, small furry ears and a tail of variable length. The average body size is from 35-45cm, including the tail. It arrived in Britain around 1714 and drove out the smaller, less adaptable Black Rats. Nowadays, the Brown Rat is the dominant species, whilst the Black Rat is found only in isolated colonies.

Fancy rats were developed from captive-bred wild rats. The principal breeder was none other than Queen Victoria's Royal Ratcatcher. Jack Black plied his trade in London during the 1840s and 1850s and, as well as destroying pests, bred natural mutations such as Blacks and Albinos, which he sold to young ladies as pets. Nowadays fancy rats are derived only from *Rattus norvegicus*. However, in recent years *Rattus rattus* has been bred by a few specialist rat fanciers. The fancy rat provides great scope as a pet and show animal and is an intelligent and loving companion.

Today's fancy rats are descended from the Brown or Norway Rat.

A SHORT HISTORY OF THE RAT FANCY

In 1901, Miss Mary Douglas, a long-time fancy rat keeper, wrote to Walter Maxey, the Secretary of the newly-formed National Mouse Club, suggesting that the NMC should lay on classes for fancy rats at their shows. Maxey agreed, and classes were first staged in Aylesbury in October 1901, where Miss Douglas won Best In Show with an 'Even Marked' rat. Many new varieties of fancy rat were developed and they became so popular that the club changed its name to the National Mouse and Rat Club. However, after Miss Douglas died in 1921, the Rat Fancy began to decline. The club reverted to the name of National Mouse Club and, in 1931, dropped support for rats altogether.

In 1974, Geoff Izzard and Joan Pearce met at a show in London where a few fancy rats were on display. They joined the London and Southern Counties Mouse Club, the only club in the UK that still staged classes for fancy rats. They showed fancy rats throughout 1975, attracting more fanciers until, on 13 January 1976, they founded the National Fancy Rat Society. The NFRS staged its first show in April 1976.

The rat fancy spread to other countries, including the USA, Sweden, Finland and Holland, and many specimens of British-bred fancy rats were exported to help establish the fancy in these countries. Later on, fancy rats of varieties not available in the UK were exported to Britain.

In April 1996, the NFRS staged its 20th Anniversary show where no less than 112 fancy rats were shown, covering every variety in existence. The Society itself now boasts over 400 members worldwide. Mary Douglas would be proud!

Fancy rats are available in many different colours and varieties, including the curly-coated Rex. This is a Himalayan Rex.

SELECTION

Before buying your first Fancy Rat, you must ask yourself the following:

- Do you want a rat as a pet, or also as a show animal?
- Do you want one or two rats, or more?
- What sex do you want your rat to be?
- What variety of rat do you want to keep?
- Do you have space to keep a rat?
- Do you have the time to give a rat the attention it needs?
- Do you want to breed from your rats? Can you find good homes for the offspring?
- If the rat is for a child, make sure that
  (a) the child wants a pet rat.
  (b) he or she will still care for it once the novelty has worn off.
  (c) he or she has permission to keep a rat.

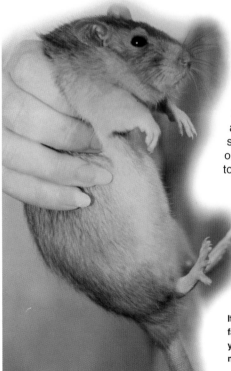

HOW TO CHOOSE YOUR PET

Before buying your rat from a pet shop, look carefully around the store. Is it clean and tidy? Are the staff interested in what they are doing? How are the animals kept? Avoid any shop where too many rats - or any animal - are cramped together in dirty, smelly cages.

Some rat fanciers advertise locally or you can get in touch with a specialist rat club which should be able to put you in touch with local rat breeders. Always visit the breeder's home

It is very important to handle a fancy rat correctly by placing your hand around its body. It must never be held by its tail.

Fancy rats can make intelligent, friendly pets, so it is important to select carefully the right rat for you.

so that you can see how the rats have been cared for. Take careful note of their environment. Do the animals have enough room to move freely? Do they look healthy? Although all Fancy Rats are born 'tame', that is, not wild, they still have to be socialised to accept human beings. Therefore, do not expect docile baby rats (kittens) but, equally, do not accept a kitten that appears terrified and bites.

Are the rats alert and interested in their surroundings? Are they skittish and darting? Are they torpid and uninterested? An uninterested rat is as bad as a skittish or aggressive one.

Mother rats are naturally protective towards their offspring, but do not buy the kittens if she seems shy or aggressive. Temperament is inherited as well as learned and your rat will take after its mother. Use the opportunity of handling a kitten to check that it is in good health. Pick it up by placing one hand over its back, sliding your fingers under the belly and carefully lifting it onto the palm of your other hand. Gently grip the base of the kitten's tail if it is nervous. You can lift small rats by holding them at the base of the tail. Never hold a rat by the tip of its tail, which may 'skin' itself or even break!

A healthy rat should be neither scrawny nor fat, although kittens do have natural puppy fat until they mature. The fur should be in good condition, bright and sleek. A rat kitten's fur is softer than an adult's, and several varieties of fancy rat are much paler as kittens.

Young rats under 13 weeks of age are known as kittens. This young fellow is a good example of the Topaz variety.

Look for scabs, bites or bald patches in the fur, and have nothing to do with a rat with any sign of parasite infestation. The eyes should be bold, clear and bright, the nose clean and free from discharge. If the rat is sneezing or wheezing, don't buy it. The ears should be erect, whole and clean. Check the tail and genital area for cleanliness. Excessive staining is a sure sign of diarrhoea. Check the tail, too, for signs of any damage or kinks. Rats with kinked tails cannot be shown and should not be bred from. The whiskers should be clean and straight, although the curly-coated Rex has naturally bent and wavy whiskers.

No rat kitten should be sold under the age of six weeks, which is the minimum weaning age. Check that the kittens are completely weaned off their mother's milk. Finally, if you are buying a female (or doe) aged over eight weeks, check that she has been separated from her brothers. The last thing you want is a young, pregnant doe.

HOW MANY RATS?

It is perfectly acceptable to have a single rat as a pet, but then you must take the place of its companions. A lonely rat can be an unhappy rat. If you want a happy and contented pet, buy two rats, but make sure that you get two of the same sex unless you want to breed.

BUCK OR DOE?

The average adult male (buck) weighs 500-600 grams, a female (doe) weighs 200-300 grams. If you want a big rat who will curl up on your lap or shoulder, choose a buck; if you want a more active, playful rat, choose a doe. Bucks often mark their territory by leaving traces of urine wherever they go. Does seldom do this. The average buck lives for about 2-2^1/$_4$ years. A doe can live up to 2^1/$_2$ years, although some rats of either sex can live for 3 to 3^1/$_2$ years.

WHAT VARIETY?

This is a matter of personal taste as there are many different colours and markings in fancy rats, not to mention all the 'crossbreeds'. If you want to exhibit, you must consider the difficulty of breeding particular varieties to show standard. Some bloodlines are more temperamental than others and you should check this with the breeder. Don't believe people who say that all show quality animals are highly strung and that all pet quality animals make excellent pets. It all comes down to bloodlines, individual rats and how the breeder looks after them.

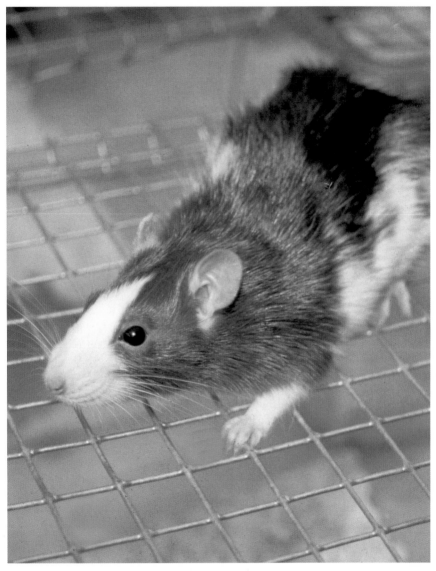

Some varieties of fancy rat, though not yet officially recognised, are still attractive and popular. This marked variety is commonly known as the Badger.

A cage should have sufficient width and length to allow the rat free movement, a good area of floor space, and be sufficiently tall that it can stand up unhindered. Rats are very active and enjoy climbing, which is good exercise for their muscles and stimulates growth in young rats. A cage too small to allow them such exercise is unsuitable. The minimum size of cage for a pair of rats is 60cm x 30cm x 30cm.

The ideal cage has a base of hard plastic or metal. Wire mesh or bars make up the main body, with glass or clear plastic forming one wall or part of one wall. The gauge of the wire or bars should be about 15mm so that the rat cannot squeeze through. Wire mesh floors are highly unsuitable for rats' feet. Aviaries can be adapted; the best size is 180cm x 90cm x 90cm, which can house several rats. You can also use an aquarium tank fitted with a sturdy wire lid, weighted down so that it cannot be pushed off.

It is important to buy the right cage for your rats. Make sure that it is big enough to house the rats and their toys.

The best floor covering (substrate) is wood shavings or sawdust purchased from a pet shop or supplier and that has been treated with disinfectant to kill germs. Untreated material may contain harmful impurities. Peat or cat litter is used sometimes, but is not ideal and can make the rats very dirty. Never use newspaper or printed paper in the cage as the print is toxic; also rats will tear it up and soil it very quickly.

The best bedding is shredded paper, preferably packaged and pre-medicated. Fresh hay helps to improve the rats' coats, acting as a sort of comb when they roll in it, and also provides a source of roughage in the diet. Ensure that the hay is clean, as badly-prepared bags can hold nettles or stones, and also parasites which will infest a rat's fur. Avoid cotton wool and man-made fibre. The hard strands can wind around a rat's throat, legs and feet, perhaps even severing its toes.

The cage should be protected from draughts, direct sunlight or excesses of temperature. Many fanciers keep their rats in an out-building, known as a rattery, which should be clean, dry and well ventilated. Heating is not necessary unless you live in a very cold area, and the rats will be warm enough with extra bedding. However, if heating is necessary, use a small electric heater or lamp. Oil and gas heaters are dangerous, especially in a wooden shed. The optimum temperature for housing rats is 15-19°C (59-66°F).

EXERCISE AND TOYS

Fancy rats enjoy being off the ground, often resting or sleeping on a perch or raised platform. You can buy thick bird perches to fit into the cage, or use branches, first making sure they are very clean. Rats enjoy gnawing so you will have to replace the perches every so often. Make small swings and platforms from chipboard and fix them onto the bars or lid of the cage. Ropes are also a favourite, and rats run up and down them with great agility. Metal bird-cage ladders can also be used.

Avoid exercise wheels, as most are too small for a rat, which could trap its tail in the spokes. Other toys include empty jam jars or a tin can with all the sharp pieces of metal removed. Rats also like pushing around small balls, such as marbles. Avoid purpose-made plastic toys, as the rats will chew them up very quickly. Rats love to chew on cardboard tubes from kitchen towel or toilet tissue rolls. Younger rats also enjoy running in and out of the tubes. Give your rats a small block of smooth wood and replace it when it has been chewed beyond recognition.

MAINTENANCE

Tidy the cage daily, removing any perishable food and clearing away any droppings. Some rats maintain a special toilet corner, making the cleaning easier. Clean out the cage once a week, replacing all sawdust and bedding. Use a triangular scraper to remove any matter stuck in the corners, which tend to accumulate the worst of a week's mess. Every three months, thoroughly wash and disinfect the cage, using a diluted disinfectant to eradicate any dirt which could lead to a build-up of germs. Wash all the cage furniture regularly.

Wood shavings make an ideal floor covering for your rat's cage.

GENERAL CARE

Fancy rats are omnivorous and quite cosmopolitan in their feeding habits. However, the rat must receive a well-balanced diet to reach and maintain a level of good health and show quality. Generally, an adult rat is fed once a day, usually in the evening when it is most active, but two smaller meals are also acceptable.

BASIC DIET

The basic diet consists of a dry food mix, obtained from a pet shop. It contains mixed corn, wheat, cereals, flaked maize, biscuit and dried, crushed peas. Avoid 'Hamster mix', as this has too many sunflower seeds and peanuts, which are very rich in protein and can cause skin problems in rats if given in excess. Mono-diets are not good for rats; they are uninteresting and many rats become bored with them and even refuse to eat them. Variety in the rat's diet is all-important. A healthy diet includes wholemeal bread, non-sugared breakfast cereals, some dog biscuit, cooked potato, rice, and table scraps such as vegetables and spaghetti. Spicy foods should not be given. A small quantity of cooked meat can be given occasionally.

Rats enjoy chewing the meat off bones and then gnawing into them to extract the marrow. This gives extra nutrition and provides good exercise for their teeth. However, avoid poultry and fish bones, which can splinter and get stuck in a rat's throat, causing injury or even death.

GREEN FOOD

Vegetables and fruit provide vitamins and additional moisture, together with all-important folic acid, which helps red blood cells to mature in the animal's bloodstream. Ideal greens are: apple, carrot, tomato, celery, cabbage, lettuce, broccoli and swede. Avoid citrus fruits and onions which are too acidic for small animals' stomachs. Give your rats green food only every second or third day and purely as a supplement to the dry diet. Do not give too much as too many greens can cause diarrhoea.

VITAMINS AND SUPPLEMENTS

Unlike man, rats can produce their own Vitamin C, so they don't need a great intake of this particular vitamin. Rats are economical feeders and practice refection: eating their droppings to ensure yet further absorption of minerals. The droppings contain naturally-produced Vitamin K, produced by bacteria in the rat's gut.

Pet shops sell vitamins and supplements and there is no harm in adding some of these to your rat's diet, although they should not be necessary if the rat is fed correctly. Preparations such as wheat germ and cod liver oil can be added to dry food. Cod liver oil is available in capsules and is greatly enjoyed by most rats. One capsule per rat per week is sufficient, but a little extra a week before a show enhances coat condition.

FOOD AND WATER

Always place your rat's food in a strong earthenware bowl that cannot be tipped over easily. It is natural for rats to scratch around for food, so sprinkle a little dry mix on the cage floor to give them something to do. Remove all perishable food within 24 hours, or it will start to go mouldy and cause bacterial build-up. Replenish the drinking water daily. This is best provided in a gravity water bottle fixed to the bars of the cage or suspended on a hanger looped over the side of a tank or hung from the lid. Water bowls may be used, but they will get dirty quite quickly.

HANDLING AND GENERAL CARE

Your rat will be stressed by being parted from its litter-mates and taken to a new home. Bring it straight home, place it in its cage with some food and water and leave it alone for a few hours. This allows the rat time to explore its new home and establish its own territory. (In the wild, rats have a condition known as 'neophobia', literally a fear of new things, and this is present to a lesser extent in fancy rats.) The rat will establish its territory by urinating or defecating in specific parts of the cage, although in future it will probably reserve a corner of the cage as a toilet area.

TAMING AND TRAINING

Start the taming process by feeding your rat and establishing a daily routine. Rats have poor eyesight, but will quickly identify you by their sense of smell. Avoid making sharp, jerky movements which will unsettle or panic the rat. Rats can transmit their fear to other rats, so be especially careful if you have more than one rat. Talk to your rat as you feed it and whenever you are near the cage and the rat will associate your voice with you, adding this to the movement and smell picture it has of you.

After a day or so, the rat should be sufficiently calm for you to attempt the next stage. Offer a tasty titbit - chocolate drops are a great favourite. The rat will sniff you and the titbit and then, if it feels confident enough, take the food from your fingers and sit down to eat it. Soon, the rat should run to meet you or stand on its hind legs when you approach the cage. Offer the rat a titbit and, while it is eating, gently bring one hand over its back and around its midriff. Carefully lift it out of the cage and place it on the palm of your other hand or on your forearm. You can pick up a young rat by the base of its tail and quickly transfer it in this way.

Sit down when handling a new rat in case it jumps from your hand. Let the rat explore, talking to it all the time and offering titbits so that it learns to come back to you. Your rat will become tame and quite bold in its explorations very quickly - it may even come when you call it, but this depends on how interesting its surroundings are compared with you!

The correct, balanced diet is all-important for your rats, especially growing kittens. Fresh drinking water should always be available and is best provided in a gravity-fed water bottle - bowls can be soiled too easily.

As the rat gets tamer let it run around the floor, but be careful that it does not chew electrical cables and cannot disappear into any nooks and crannies. Some rats gnaw their way into sofas and armchairs from below and then stubbornly refuse to come out. If the rat defecates where it shouldn't, pick it up (along with the faeces if they are dry) and place both back in the cage with a simple admonishment. The rat will soon learn to return to its cage to relieve itself.

Eventually, the rat should be tame enough to be allowed to run around the room when the cage is open. There is no set time limit for exercise; it is all a matter of what suits the individual rat and owner. Some rats explore for a few minutes then happily snuggle down on their owners' shoulders.

Rats can be taught all sorts of tricks. The key to teaching your rat to perform any trick is twofold: patience and food. The rat will do nothing unless there is something in it for the rat, so have plenty of treats handy. The easiest trick is to train your rat to run up a small ladder and retrieve a titbit from your hand. Next, construct a maze out of cardboard or plastic tubes and boxes, creating walls and corridors for the rat to run down to find its reward. You must remember that, like people, all rats are different. Some individuals will respond better to training than others, so don't expect too much too soon and you won't be disappointed.

With gentle persuasion and patience, fancy rats can become very tame and will enjoy being handled.

SHOWING

If you want to show, first contact the fancy rat organisation in your area. In the UK, this is the National Fancy Rat Society, while there are several localised rat groups in the United States. The secretaries continually change but write to me, c/o TFH Publications, enclosing an s.a.e. or International Reply Coupon, and I will try to put you in touch with the appropriate fancy rat organisation.

Do not despair if your rat is not a top quality show rat. Most rat groups stage classes for 'pet quality' rats, which are judged on their condition and tameness rather than on the variety standard. It is well worth joining a fancy rat group, as this provides good social contact with like-minded people, and information about the cares and pleasures of keeping fancy rats is shared between members.

GENERAL CONFORMATION AND STANDARDS OF EXCELLENCE

Every Fancy Rat is judged to the **General Conformation**, which relates to its type, size, shape and physique. The General Conformation of a Fancy Rat reads as follows:

The rat shall be of good size, does long and racy in build, bucks being of a bigger build, arched over the loin, firm fleshed, with clean, long head, but not too pointed at the nose. The eyes shall be bold, clean and of good size. The ears shall be of good size, well formed and widely spaced. The tail shall be cylindrical and as long as the body, thick at the base, tapering to a fine point. The ears, tail and feet shall be covered with fine hair. The coat shall be smooth and glossy (except the Rex type). Bucks are larger than does and have a harsher coat.

Each variety is judged to a **Standard of Excellence**, which is a description and set of points relating to that variety. All rats of a particular variety compete against each other to determine the best specimen of that variety. Then the winning rats compete to win Best Rat In Show. Rats that have severe scabs, mites or fleas, lack of whiskers, obvious ill-health or which are intractable are disqualified.

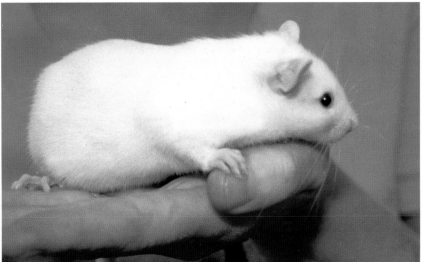

Above: It is a very enjoyable experience to exhibit your fancy rat at a show.
Below: A pert, hopeful show rat. This is a Black Eyed White.

VARIETIES

There is not room to list the individual scale of points for each variety. Only the British names and descriptions have been used because a number of varieties go under different names in different countries or even between different groups. All the standards here relate to *Rattus norvegicus*.

Selfs: Self rats have one overall body colour, and are divided into two sub-groups: Dark Eyed and Red Eyed. The Dark Eyed specimens relate to Self rats with one body colour and includes Black Eyed White, Black, Chocolate, Mink (a mid-grey coloured rat), and a recently-developed variety, Blue, which is a 'deep, steel blue', the fur being blue-grey down to the skin. As yet, the Blue does not have a full standard, but what is classed as a 'guide standard', putting it at an interim stage between a new, unstandardised variety and a fully-recognised standardised variety. The Red Eyed sub-group includes Pink Eyed White (commonly called Albino, a very common mutation) and Champagne, which is a warm beige tone. There is a guide standard variety called Buff, which is an even, warm magnolia, with ruby eyes.

Marked: The Marked varieties are the most difficult to breed to conform fully to a standard. Berkshire is a long-established variety, which has a standard coloured body, with a white belly, which should be as symmetrically marked as possible, white feet and, in darker specimens, the tail white to half its length. The Irish is more difficult to breed correctly, being a standard coloured rat with a white equilateral triangle on its chest. The most popular Marked variety is the Hooded, which has a coloured 'hood' covering the head, throat, chest and shoulders, and a stripe called the 'saddle' extending down its back in an unbroken line. The saddle should range between 0.75cm and 1.25cm in width. In darker coloured Hoodeds, the saddle should extend halfway down the tail. Capped is also popular, although again difficult to breed correctly. The rat has a coloured 'cap', which follows the lower jaw line and should not extend past the ears. It has a blaze on its face which should be enclosed within the cap itself. Variegated is a very attractive rat with a coloured head and shoulders, ideally with a white blaze on the forehead. The rest of the body should be white, with coloured variegation over the back and flanks, not extending down to the belly.

Silvered: This group contains rats of any recognised coat colour with a proliferation of silver guard hairs within their coats; that is, individual hairs tipped with silver giving an overall silvery sheen. Silvered black rats are known as Silver Grey. Other popular Silvers are Silver Mink, Silver Chocolate and Silver Cinnamon. Silver Fawn is one of the oldest and most popular varieties. It is a rich orange fawn on top, ticked with silver guard hairs, and a pure white belly. The demarcation line between the top and belly colour should be clear and sharp. The eyes are red, as basically the rat is devoid of dark pigment. Topaz is a recently-developed colour, similar to a Silver Fawn but more 'golden fawn' in colour with a blue/grey undercolour to the skin. The belly fur is silver and the eyes are dark ruby.

Any Other Variety: This group contains rats not included in any other group, including Agouti, the so-called 'wild' rat colour, a rich, ruddy brown ticked with black guard hairs. The Cinnamon is a warm russet-brown, evenly ticked with chocolate guard hairs. It is most attractive but quite difficult to breed correctly. Himalayan is also a difficult variety to breed to standard. It has a white body, with dark coloured patches (points), on its face, from nose to eyes, ears, tail, feet, forelegs and hindlegs. The eyes are distinctly red. Siamese is a variety which developed out of Himalayan and has a medium beige body colour, shading darker towards the tail. It also has distinct points on its face, ears, tail, feet, forelegs and hindlegs. Its eyes are ruby coloured. Pearl is a very attractive variety, coloured the palest silver shading to a creamish undercolour, the fur delicately tipped with grey over the whole animal. It has distinct black eyes. Cinnamon Pearl has no less than three distinct bands of colour, namely cream, blue and orange, with silver guard hairs giving an overall golden appearance with a silver sheen. The belly fur is pale silver grey, setting off the top colour nicely. Bold black eyes add to the overall effect.

Rex: Rex rats have curly coats which must be dense, evenly curled and with as few guard hairs as possible. The Rex also has curly whiskers. Rexes tend to appear thicker-set than smooth coated varieties. A Rex can conform to any recognised coat colour or pattern, although to show a marked Rex, such as a Hooded, is a double challenge, as the rat is judged by its marking conformation as well as the curliness of the Rex coat.

Note the curly whiskers of the Himalayan Rex in the foreground as opposed to the long, straight whiskers of the smooth coated rat behind.

Unstandardised Varieties: The NFRS has very strict criteria for the recognition of new varieties. The rats must breed true, that is, rats of the same variety must produce offspring of that variety. Also, unstandardised rats must gain first placings under a number of different judges in the special Unstandardised classes. At the moment many new varieties are vying for recognition, including the Lilac, a paler version of the Mink to which it is closely related; the Badger, a marked variety with a coloured body and head, the face being 'split' by a blaze rather like that of a badger; and most recently, the Chinchilla, which has a white base to its coat, with a blue undercoat and black ticking.

General Conformation, description of varieties and extracts from Standards © NFRS 1996

Mis-marked fancy rats can still compete in special Pet Rat classes, where they are judged on their condition and tameness.

The head of a fancy rat should be long, but not too pointed at the nose.

This kitten is a good example of the popular Siamese variety.

BREEDING

Fancy rats can be extremely prolific, but it is cruel to allow them to breed indiscriminately. First, consider these issues:

- Do you have enough cages for a breeding project? You will need one cage for each buck and doe, one for the buck after mating and at least one cage for the offspring once they are weaned.
- Can you find homes for the surplus kittens?
- Are you hoping to make money from selling rat kittens? Forget it! Unless you own a special rodent breeding farm, you will never get rich from breeding rats.
- Finally, especially for the younger reader: obtain your parents' permission before you start a rat breeding programme!

GENETICS

Genetics is the science of heredity. Ask advice from more experienced fanciers as to what varieties should be mated and what the results of the pairing will be, and listen to what they tell you. Never breed from two rats with the same fault as this then becomes genetically 'fixed' in the offspring. Both rats should be in good health and be good examples of the breed. The primary requirements in breeding are good husbandry and an eye for a good specimen.

MATING AND GESTATION

A doe has a five-day oestrus cycle, so every five days she will be receptive to mating. A doe on heat tends to be jumpy and excitable. If touched on her flanks, she may adopt a passive stance, ready for mating. Often, a discharge is visible from her vulva. Put the buck and doe into a small cage with a little food, leave them to mate overnight, and separate them the next morning.

You can house the buck and doe in a normal cage and leave them for a week or two, during which time the doe will come into heat and they will mate. Sometimes, the rats take a little time to get acquainted, sleeping at either end of the cage. Eventually the doe should show the first signs of pregnancy: a distinct swelling of the abdomen which, when viewed from above, gives her an almost pear-shaped appearance. Now the pair should be split up, to allow the doe to prepare for the birth.

On average, rat gestation (pregnancy) lasts between 21 and 23 days. Keep the doe as quiet as possible, restrict her exercise and give her extra food and bread and milk to nourish the growing embryos. A few days before the birth, clean the cage thoroughly, and put in plenty of clean shavings and bedding material.

Two or three pregnant does can litter together, as long as the babies are due at about the same time. Sometimes, two nursing does make a communal nest and suckle all the kittens together. House the does separately if you want to be sure which kittens belong to which doe.

THE LITTER

The doe starts to build the nest furiously and takes little interest in her food. A pinkish discharge indicates the beginning of the birth. The doe squats on her haunches and the kittens are born one by one, each in its own uterine sac. The doe bites open each sac and nips off the umbilical cord. She washes each kitten, which stimulates its breathing and bodily functions.

Between seven to ten kittens are born, and younger does usually have smaller first litters. The kittens are born blind, deaf and naked. They emit high pitched squeaks so that the doe can find them easily. The kittens quickly seek out the doe's nipples and start to suckle. This first feed is vital as they receive passive immunity to infection through antibodies in the mother's milk.

The doe becomes sexually receptive immediately after giving birth (post partum oestrus) which is why the buck is removed before the litter is born. To be pregnant whilst rearing a litter would place great physical strain on the doe and, almost certainly, the new kittens would be very small and weak. The doe should be allowed to rest for about a month before being mated again. Does are sexually active until 14 months of age, bucks for slightly longer.

It is rare for does to eat their litters but they will eat kittens that are either already dead or very sickly. It is not true that bucks eat kittens. A buck will make a good father and nest with the kittens whilst the doe is resting if he is left with the doe.

Do not handle the kittens until two or three days after they are born and always rub your hands in the bedding to acquire the 'nest smell'. The kittens develop rapidly. Their fur begins to grow within a day of birth, and markings on the Capped and Hooded varieties are visible within four or five days.

By ten days, the kittens are fully furred, their ears have opened and their incisor teeth have broken through. Now they start to nibble at solid

A female rat, known as a doe, will give birth to a litter averaging six to eight kittens. She will suckle these for up to six weeks, after which they may be weaned and separated from her.

food, which the doe brings into the nest for them. The kittens' eyes open at 14 days and they begin to explore the cage, finding food for themselves. Bread and milk is a healthy, nutritious supplement to the main dry diet and the mother's milk.

The kittens grow quickly and indulge in madcap games of play fighting. This helps them to create their own 'pecking order', as dominance plays a great part in rat hierarchy. Grooming is a peaceful way of enforcing dominance over more submissive individuals. Mock mating sometimes takes place, which is another stage of the kittens' social development. Handle the kittens as regularly as possible to instil tameness.

GROWING UP

At six weeks the kittens are ready to be weaned. Remove them to a suitable cage and provide plenty of toys and distractions. Give them bread and milk, and plenty of food and water. Kittens may need feeding more than twice a day; check what food is left after each feed and adjust subsequent feeds accordingly. Gradually reduce the bread and milk until it is cut out completely.

Now you can select the best show quality kittens, but remember that some varieties take longer to develop their true show potential. Many varieties retain a drab, greyish tinge to their naturally softer, downy 'baby coat' until the first moult takes place, which occurs between the ages of six and eleven weeks. Also, some varieties tend not to show well as kittens.

Separate the kittens into single-sex groups before they become sexually mature at the age of eight weeks. The best way to differentiate the sexes is to check the distance between the urethra and the anus, which is noticeably closer in does than in bucks. Does have two rows of nipples which are usually quite obvious. A buck has testicles, although these only 'drop' outside the body when he is hot or sexually aroused.

Finally, you must ensure that surplus kittens go to good homes. Make sure that the new owner is aware of the rat's needs and has the necessary equipment. If you sell your rats to a pet shop, the kittens' final destination is in the hands of the shop assistants. All you can do is to make sure that the pet shop is clean and well maintained and that the staff know what they are talking about.

HEALTH

A complete list of ailments and their treatment is impossible so the following is a list of the major ailments that afflict fancy rats. The keys to successful pet health care are good husbandry, good diet and regular exercise. If in doubt, see a vet!

Wounds and abscesses: A deep wound exposing muscle tissue needs to be sutured within six hours or the skin begins to die and treatment will be

Fancy rats are generally very hardy animals but good care is needed to prevent serious ailments.

difficult. Bathe a shallow wound with warm water, then apply iodine. Repeat this twice a day for two or three days until a scab develops and new skin forms. If an abscess develops, gently squeeze out the pus with tissue or cotton wool and then bathe the area with warm water. Apply a drop of hydrogen peroxide to force the remaining pus out of the cavity. Continue the process of 'flush and drain' daily until all the pus is gone and a scab forms over new flesh.

Colds: The symptoms of colds are a staring (fluffed up) coat, a general hunched appearance and discharge from the eyes and nose, often red in colour. The rat will also sneeze and wheeze. Isolate the rat in a smaller cage and keep it warm. Give it extra food, such as a warm mash, and plenty to drink. An untreated cold can develop into pneumonia, when the rat's breathing becomes heavier and it loses weight rapidly. Go to your vet, as antibiotics will be required.

Diarrhoea: Diarrhoea is also known as scours. Loose, pale and runny droppings indicate diarrhoea, which probably is caused by too much green food. Provide a dry food diet for a few days before gradually increasing the rat's intake of green food. If diarrhoea recurs, cut out all food and give rice water - that is, unsalted water in which rice has been boiled. Liquid charcoal also helps to stabilise the rat's gut. Feed the rat on bread and milk for a few days, then gradually return to the usual diet. Diarrhoea can also be caused by infections of the gut. A course of antibiotics and a dry food diet will generally correct the problem in this case.

Dehydration: Dehydration is a side effect of an illness and rats can also get badly dehydrated whilst suffering from diarrhoea, because of the sudden loss of bodily fluids. Symptoms are rapid weight loss, hunched up appearance, staring coat and lower body temperature. Gently pinch the rat's scruff: if the skin lacks elasticity and does not revert to its normal shape, then the rat is dehydrated. If it shows no interest in food or water you must take a pipette and force some water mixed with glucose into its mouth. Do not do this too forcefully, as the liquid could run back through the rat's nostrils and choke it. The rat should perk up once it gets fluid back into its system.

Mites: These minute skin-dwelling parasites can cause bald patches in the rat's fur, together with spots and scabs on the skin. Buy an anti-mite solution from the vet, dip the rat into it and the mites usually die quickly. Serious mite infestations, such as demodectic mange, require veterinary treatment.

Fancy rats are gregarious animals and enjoy company. Ideally, it is best to keep a pair of rats of the same sex as company for each other.

Two well-cared-for rats in tip-top condition.

Fancy rats can be the ideal pet for people of all ages.

Spots and sores: Spots and sores can also be caused by diet. Too many sunflower seeds or peanuts cause an excess of protein to form in the rat's body, causing skin inflammation. The rat scratches the sores and makes them worse. Give the rat cooked rice, bread and vegetables and add some Vitamin B to its drinking water. Treat the spots and sores with a simple animal antiseptic ointment. After a few days, the rat can go back to its usual diet - minus the protein-rich items.

Respiratory infections: The first symptoms are sneezing and a discharge from the nose. The most dreaded rat infection is called snuffles, a bacterial infection which causes the rat to wheeze and 'rattle' as it develops a sinus and/or chest infection. Untreated snuffles can lead to pneumonia. Isolate any rat with a respiratory ailment as a matter of course.

Tumours: Unfortunately, rats are susceptible to tumours, especially in later life. Tumours are often genetic in origin, so discontinue breeding from a bloodline of rats prone to them. Benign tumours are quite soft to the touch and are generally harmless. Even so, they can grow very large and become painful for the rat. The tumour can be surgically removed and, in most cases, the rat will make a full recovery. However, if further tumours develop, the rat should be put to sleep rather than subjected to further surgery. Malignant tumours grow faster than benign tumours. They are hard to the touch and attached firmly to underlying bodily tissues. Such tumours are cancerous and there is no kindness in having them removed, as the cancer will spread and affect other parts of the body. The rat will suffer a great deal of discomfort, so it is kinder to put it to sleep.

OLD AGE

You must treat an old rat gently and with respect, and not subject it to stress and noise. Fancy Rats make excellent pets and will repay your care with genuine affection. Your first Fancy Rat may have a short life but, hopefully, it will be a full and happy one.

BIBLIOGRAPHY

RATS
Susan Fox
ISBN 0-87666-933-X
KW-128

This book, of particular value to beginners, presents sensible, easy-to-follow information about selecting and caring for pet rats.
Hardcover: 130mm x 200mm, 96 pages, more than 75 colour photos and drawings

RATS FOR THOSE WHO CARE
Dennis Kelsey-Wood
ISBN 0-7938-1392-1
B-114

This attractive book is aimed at beginners, giving the basics of starting off in fancy rat keeping. It covers such areas as accommodation, selection, food, breeding and exhibition, and health care.
Softcover: 174mm x 212mm, 32 pages, illustrated throughout with colour photos

THE PROPER CARE OF FANCY RATS
Nick Mays
ISBN 0-86622-340-1
TW-122

This book provides the reader with all the basics of fancy rat ownership, from selecting the right animal to providing the best feeding, housing and healthcare. There is also valuable guidance on breeding and showing fancy rats.
Hardcover: 122mm x 174mm, 256 pages, illustrated throughout with colour photos

GUIDE TO OWNING A RAT
Susan Fox
ISBN 0-7938-2157-6
RE 508

Softcover: 170mm x 250mm, 64 pages, illustrated throughout with full colour individually laminated photos.

For information about the National Fancy Rat Society write to the author care of T.F.H. Publications, PO Box 15 Waterlooville PO7 6BQ, enclosing a stamped addressed envelope or an international reply coupon (if outside the United Kingdom).